A GUIDE TO FACEBOOK ADVERTISING

I0510571

Chris J. Brodie

A GUIDE TO

facebook

ADVERTISING

Chris J. Brodie

A GUIDE TO FACEBOOK ADVERTISING

Copyright ©2019 by Chris J. Brodie

All rights reserved.

No part of this publication may be reproduced, stored in a retrieval system, or transmitted in any form or by any means, electronic, mechanical, photocopying, recording, or otherwise without the prior written permission of the author, with the exception of brief excerpts in magazine, articles, and critical reviews.

Table of Contents

CHAPTER ONE: INTRODUCTION

"Every business needs a Facebook's presence," you probably may have heard this many times, and it's indeed true. Facebook may have started as a social network to connect people, but presently it's arguably the biggest advertising platform. Facebook kick started an advertising revolution, let's put things in perspective:

> Facebook has over 2.33 billion active monthly
> users and 1.56 billion daily active users, that's
> more than the population of China, five times the
> population of the United States, and 20% of the
> world's population. An average user spends about
> an hour each day on Facebook. It's massive user
> base provides Facebook with a trove of data, data

What this means for advertisers is that you can advertise and sell your products or services to a targeted global audience. Facebook has taken its advertising platform a step further, by providing advertisers with an array of tools necessary to provide successful results or campaigns.

You may be asking yourself, "why do I need Facebook Ads?"

For starters, you are not only in the 21st century but also living in a fast paced technological era where virtually the entire world communicates via social media, and Facebook happens to be the biggest of them all. Add to that the fact that we are in an advertising crazy era where all companies (big/small), and also independent marketers and producers are constantly selling to a global audience using not the old traditional medium of advertising but digital advertising. So, to answer your question, *"you will be cutting yourself short and will never meet your sales goals if you don't jump on the Facebook advertising train."*

IMPORTANCE OF FACEBOOK ADVERTISING

Facebook advertising is the primary digital medium used to grow businesses. Here are 5 why reasons Facebook advertising is so important:

1. It has a massive user base

   As highlighted earlier, Facebook has 1.56 billion daily active users and a 2.56 billion monthly active users. What this means is that you have a global audience (20% of the world's population) to promote and sell your business (products or services) to.

2. It's cost-effective

   With all the benefits it brings, one would expect that placing ads on Facebook would be expensive, but on the contrary, it cost-effective and budget friendly – anyone or business can afford to place ads of Facebook.

3. You have access to a targeted audience

   Just because it has a massive user base, it doesn't mean everyone will want to purchase your product or service. Having so much user data, Facebook uses laser-precision targeting to provide you with the specific type of audience you need; audience that are more likely to turn to your customer. Adding to that, Facebook takes this targeting a step further by providing you with a feature called audience insights.

4. Facebook gives you access to advertise on multiple platforms

   Facebook has a platform called Audience Network, these are Facebook partners that let you advertise on their apps and websites. Also, Facebook lets you advertise on its mobile news feed, right column, and desktop news feed, as well as Instagram new feed and Stories.

5. Facebook has a large mobile audience

An article on Time magazine that Messenger, Facebook, and Instagram are among the top 10 frequently downloaded apps on mobiles. As many people access these apps through mobiles than desktops it makes Facebook the platform to beat when it comes to mobile audience.

DIGITAL ADVERTISING IN 2019

Digital advertising also known as internet advertising is when businesses leverage the internet to promote and sell their products and services to consumers. It's delivered through email, websites, social media platforms, banner ads, search engines etc. For the last 19 years, digital advertising has been the best and most successful way to reach existing and new customers. Facebook advertising is one of the various mediums through which digital advertising is accomplished. In 2019, or since the Facebook era began, digital advertising via Facebook has been a potent medium to reach various demographics. Facebook advertising offers a lots of benefits and advantages over other forms of digital and traditional advertising: it lets you reach your audience at a low price, if you advertise on Facebook, you also have the opportunity to advertise on other social platforms such as Instagram, WhatsApp, Messenger and the Audience Network. Facebook's not the only big player in the world of digital advertising, other big players are Google and Bing Ads.

Google, Facebook and Bing are great advertising tools which helps advertisers reach targeted audiences. They all can be categorized as paid search or paid social. With paid search, you get to advertise in various platforms (most especially search engines). But you pay each time your ad is clicked on or when your ad is displayed – in paid search, prospective customers can only view your ad if they type in keywords related to your product or service in browsers or search engines. Paid search works differently, would be customers cannot search for your ad on a social platform like Facebook, rather they can only view your ad hen it appears in their feed. As you create your ad, you set your ad budget and the duration you would want your ad to run. You may be thinking, *"well Facebook users don't go on Facebook thinking of making a purchase."* And you are right, paid social has a zero purchase intent. But Facebook as been able to collect a massive trove of data from users, data relating to their interests, site activity, purchasing habits and much more. This is what make Facebook a great advertising and purchasing ad space.

UNDERSTANDING A FACEBOOK AD?

Before getting into the business of Facebook Advertising, it's important you understand that there are several types of ads one can place on Facebook:

Ads

As the name suggests, these are basically ads placed on the Facebook platform. When placing an ad, you will select your objective, placements, budget, target audience and format. You can choose from a variety of ad formats such as: carousel, video, image and a single image, and also choose to place your ad not just on Facebook but also Instagram and Audience Network.

Boosted Posts

Boosted Posts are your regular posts which you post via a business page, but it differs from a regular post by the fact that you have to pay to show to the target audience.

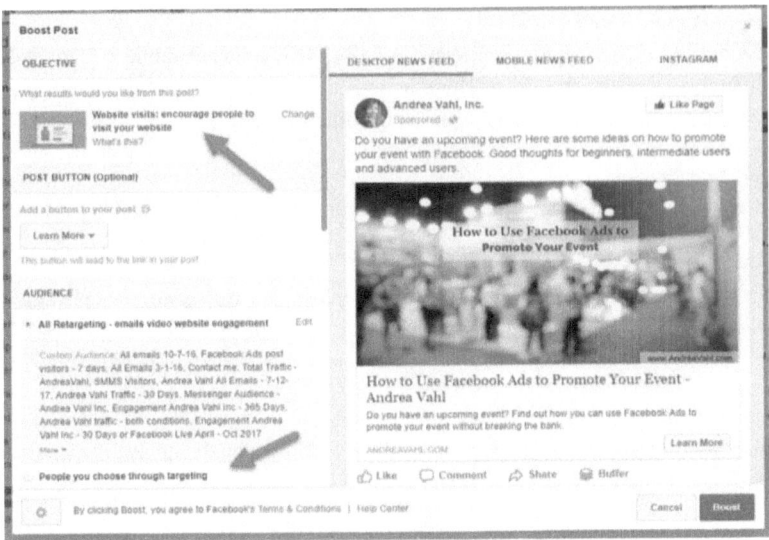

This target audience may or may not be your follower. Boosted Posts would appear in the audience's feed for a specified amount of time. When boosting a post, you simply make a post as you would regularly do, then pay Facebook to turn the post into an ad.

Stories

Facebook stories are types of ads which are 10-15 seconds full-screen videos. They appear between Instagram/ Facebook Stories, and are visible for 24 hours after which they disappear.

KEY FACEBOOK ADVERTISING TERMS

When you begin placing ads on Facebook, you will see some terms which you should know be familiar with, some key terms are:

Bid

It's an amount paid for an ad to be displayed.

Call-to-Action (CTA)
CTA buttons urge users to take a specific action. This action could be to learn more, call now, sign up, or shop now. These buttons would send users to the landing page or, in case your ad is the Lead Ad, to the pre-filled form.

Audience Network
It's a program which lets you put ads in the apps and sites of Facebook's partners.

Cost Per Acquisition (CPA)
This is an advertising technique where advertisers pay for specific acquisition or actions. CPA is based on your budget, you can adjust the price you'll like to pay for each acquisition, and Facebook will adjust your ad and its delivery accordingly.

Engagement
This simply is an action that occurs on some ad, they include: clicks, likes, views, shares, and comments.

Facebook Pixel
A piece of JavaScript code which tracks a user's action on your site.

Frequency
The average number of times an ad is displayed on Facebook.

News Feed
This is a continuous updated list of Facebook status updates, posts, & ads.

Negative Feedback
Users can carry out unwanted actions like hiding disturbing ads, selecting not to view your ads or reporting ads as spam

Objective
This is an action that you want your users to take when they view your ad.

Optimized Bidding
It's a bidding option which lets advertisers optimize their bid & delivery for certain objective.

Placement
An area where the ad appears – it could be, News Feed, in-stream videos, right column, Audience Network, and Instagram feed and Stories.

Positive Feedback
The number of times the potential audience makes some desired action including sharing, converting or liking.

Reach
It's the number of users viewing your ad.

Relevance Score
It's a metric which estimates in real time the relevance of an ad to its audience. Ads with high relevance scores appear to the audience more than the ads having fewer relevance scores.

Targeting
A set of particular descriptions that you use for describing the users whom you actually want to view your ads. It's a combination of locations, interests, demographics, and behaviors.

User
The user is an individual who uses networking websites regularly like Facebook, Snapchat, or Twitter.

A general misconception I see amongst many Facebook advertisers is the belief that Facebook will generate millions of dollars overnight as though it's some lottery. Such misconception could be traced down to internet marketers and business owners who claim or I should say boast about achieving mind blowing results from their Facebook ads, and they do this just to make newbies to Facebook marketing or individuals looking to make some dollars online purchase their courses.

Is it possible to make a ton of cash from the results of your Facebook ads? Yes! I have seen this happen many times. But for a large percentage of people who are into Facebook marketing, it's likely you won't hit the Facebook lottery. This is not to dissuade you from using Facebook advertising, but to let you know you'll need to put in some hard work to achieve positive results or get large profits.

If you need to grow your business and increase your reach via advertising, you can achieve this using Facebook advertising. If you want to grow your business, but you are confused regarding the right platform or medium to use, this book is for you.

CHAPTER TWO: FIRST STEPS IN FACEBOOK MARKETING

When you decide to advertise on Facebook, the first thing you'll need is a Facebook account, Facebook page(s) and a business manager account. In this chapter, I'll guide you on the process of creating an Instagram account, a Facebook profile, business manager account and a Facebook page.

CREATE A FACEBOOK ACCOUNT

Follow the below steps to sign up to Facebook and set up your profile:

1. Go to https://www.facebook.com. In the **"Create an account"** section, enter your information and click **Sign Up**. Take note of the email you use when signing up, because be getting important notifications regarding any as campaigns.

2. Edit your profile

3. Upload a photo

CREATE YOUR BUSINESS PAGE

The next step is creating a Facebook page – this would act as your business page. It is crucial to have a Facebook page because every ad you create will have to be linked to a Facebook page.

1. Log into your Facebook account, on the menu items next to the search bar select **"create page"**.

2. Select a page type, it could be "Brand or business" or a "Community or public figure".

3. Input a page name and category – while selecting your category, you can write 1 to 2 words which best describes your page. After that hit **"continue"**.

4. Upload a profile picture for your page – preferably, use a logo so users will associate that page with your business as this appears in the relevant search results.

5. Add a cover photo – according to Facebook, pages with cover photos get more page likes and visits, also it will make your business page appear professional.

While you'll be placing ads on Facebook, I'll also recommend creating an Instagram account so as to run ads as well. If you already have an Instagram account, you can skip this next part.

CREATE AN INSTAGRAM ACCOUNT

1. Download the Instagram app.
2. Enter a valid phone number or email to sign up.
3. Enter your full name and password.
4. Upload a profile photo.
5. Insert your contacts.
6. Connect your Facebook account.
7. Open settings and sign up for the business profile – insert business name, email and password.
8. Now, connect to a Facebook page.

CREATE AN AD ACCOUNT

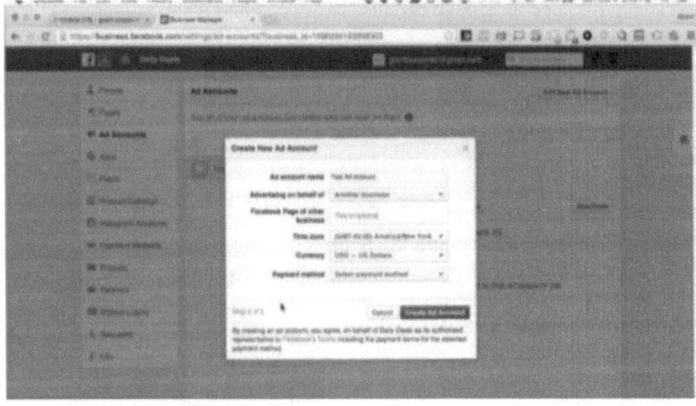

1. Go to Add and Click a "New Ad Account".

2. Now, fill the required fields. Press Create Ad Account.

3. Add people to the account and choose the account roles.

There's a limit to the number of ad accounts you can create; the maximum number is four.

CREATE A BUSINESS MANAGER

When you begin to manage several ad accounts and pages, you should sign up for a Business Manager account. A business manager is a tool that helps you organize and manage your business.

1. Visit business.facebook.com and click **"CREATE ACCOUNT"**.

2. Enter your business and account name, and also your email address.

3. Next fill in your business details.

4. And finally, you will have to transfer your assets that you want to handle under this account. Common assets are Instagram accounts, pages and other ad accounts.

Once you've created your Business Manager, you can now add your business page(s) so you can manage all of them in one place. Before you can add a page, you must be an admin, if you are not an admin you will have to request access to it.

To add a page to Business Manager:

1. In Business Manager, navigate to **Business settings — Accounts — Pages.**

2. Click + **ad**

3. Select **Add a page**

4. Enter your Facebook page or URL

You can share access to your Facebook Ad account with a partner, most especially when you are collaborating on projects or business. To connect with a partner, you have to give access to your ad account – to share access to your ad account:

Copy the ad account ID located in the Ad Accounts tab of your Business Settings (click Business Settings, Accounts and then Ad Accounts) – the ID is next to your account name. Now, you could send your ID copy to the partner, who would use this for adding you to an account. There are 2 methods you could use to connect with your partner: you might request access (through the business ID or via sending the link) or you can claim ad account of your partner.

REQUESTING ACCESS VIA BUSINESS ID

1. Select ad accounts.
2. Choose the ad account and press **"Assign Partner"**.
3. Press "Connect Your Ad Account Using Your Partner's Business ID Instead".
4. Select account role, insert business ID, & press Connect – the partner would get an alert regarding access to their account.

SENDING LINK

1. Choose a role.
2. Copy the link and close - you'll send this link to your partner.

CLAIMING AD ACCOUNT

Claiming an ad account differs from requesting access. When you claim an ad account, you're claiming full ownership of the account. When you request access to an ad account, you aren't taking that account away from its owner.

To claim an ad account:

1. Click Accounts. Go to Ad Accounts and Add. Then, Request Access to the Ad Account.
2. Insert ad account ID. Select an ad account role. Press Confirm.

For every ad account you create, you can assign roles. To assign roles:

1. Choose an Ad accounts and press Add People.
2. Select one person and assign them a role, then press Save Changes.

Now add your Instagram account to Business Manager:

1. Select Accounts and Instagram Accounts
2. Cheese + Add button.

3. Insert username and password for the Instagram accounts that you manage

In Business Manager, you view and update ad account settings, edit account information and notification settings as well as view, add, or remove ad account roles.

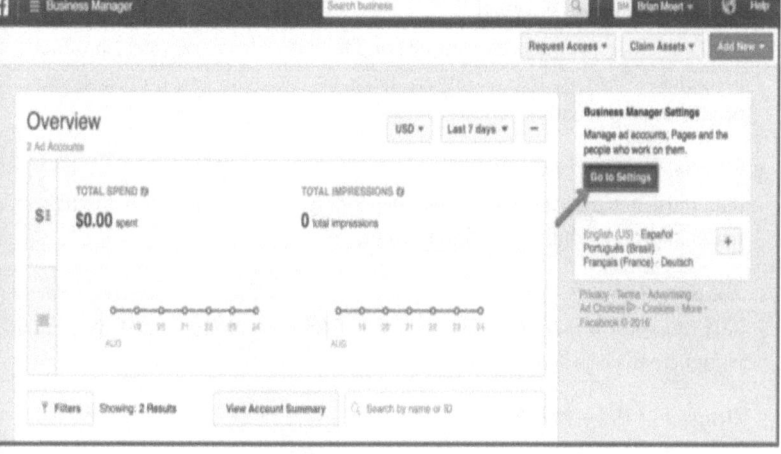

CHAPTER THREE: FACEBOOK A GUIDELINES POLICIES

When placing ads on Facebook or Instagram, ensure you abide by Facebook's ad policies. All ads placed on Facebook have to go through a review and approval process it. Facebook would review your ad to see if it abides to its policies – it checks your landing page, ad image, positioning, text and targeting. It takes 24 hours for a review. Once an ad has been reviewed, you'll be sent a notification email on the approval status of your ad.

Ads that do not abide to Facebook's policies are rejected. When an ad is rejected, reasons for rejection are always given. So, you should edit your ad according to the reasons given for rejection. To avoid confusion and delays, you should read Facebook's advertising policies some of which will be mentioned in this chapter.

PROHIBITED CONTENT

1. ***Community Standards***

   Ads should adhere to Facebook Community Standards. And ads on Instagram should not violate Instagram Community Guidelines.

2. ***Illegal Services or Products***

   Ads must not promote, constitute, or facilitate illegal services, products, or activities. Ads targeted to minors must not promote inappropriate services, products, or content.

3. ***Discriminatory Practices***

   Ads must not discriminate people depending on personal attributes like race, national origin, ethnicity, religion, color, and more.

4. ***Tobacco Products***

   Ads must not promote the use or sale of tobacco products and other related paraphernalia.

5. ***Drugs and Drug-Related Products***

   Ads should not promote the use or sale of prescription, illegal, or recreational drugs.

6. *Unsafe Supplements*

Ads should not promote the use or sale of unsafe supplements.

7. *Ammunition, Weapons, or Explosives*

Ads should not promote use or sale of ammunition, weapons, or explosives.

8. *Adult Services or Products*

Ads should not promote the use or sale of adult services or products, except for the ads for contraception and family planning.

9. *Adult Content*

Ads should not have adult content including nudity, depiction of the people in suggestive or explicit positions, and activities which are suggestive and sexually provocative.

10. *Third-Party Infringement*

Ads should not have content which violates rights of third parties, that includes privacy, copyright, publicity, trademark, and proprietary or personal rights.

11. *Sensational Content*

Ads should not contain disrespectful, shocking, excessively violent, or sensational content.

12. *Personal Attributes*

Ads should not have content which implies or asserts personal attributes.

13. *False or Misleading Content*

Ads, business practices, and landing pages shouldn't contain false, deceptive, & misleading content, such as deceptive offers, claims, & methods.

14. *Controversial Content*

Ads should not have content which exploits controversial social or political issues for commercial aims.

15. *Non-Functional Landing Pages*

Ads should not direct individuals to non-functional landing pages, this includes landing pages with content that interferes with the user's ability to actually navigate away from a page.

16. **Surveillance Equipment**

Ads must not encourage the sale of mobile trackers, spy cams, or hidden surveillance tools.

17. **Grammar and Profanity**

Ads might not contain bad or profanity grammar & punctuation. Letters, symbols, and numbers should be properly used.

18. **Nonexistent Functionality**

Ads might not have images which show non-existent functionality.

19. **Personal Health**

Ads must not have "before-&-after" images and images which contain unlikely or unexpected results. Ads for weight loss, health, or fitness products should be targeted to individuals 18 plus.

20. **Cash Advance Loans**

Ads must not encourage paycheck advances, payday loans, or other short-term loans intended to actually cover somebody's expenditures until the next payday.

21. **Multilevel Marketing**

Ads that promote income opportunities should describe the business model or product, and must also not encourage business models giving fast compensation for the small investment.

22. **Penny Auctions**

Ads might not encourage bidding fee auctions, penny auctions, and similar businesses.

23. **Counterfeit Documents**

Ads must not encourage fake documents.

24. **Disruptive or Low Quality Content**

Ads may not have content that leads to external landing pages which offer a disruptive or unexpected experience.

25. *Malware or Spyware*

Ads might not have malware, spyware, or some software which results in a deceptive or unexpected experience.

26. *Automatic Animation*

Ads may not have audio and flash animation which automatically plays without an individual's interaction.

27. *Unauthorized Streaming Devices*

Ads might not promote items or products which facilitate unauthorized access to the digital media.

28. *Circumventing Systems*

Ads should not contain tactics for circumventing the ad reviewing process and other enforcement systems.

29. *Illegal Financial Products & Services*

Ads might not encourage financial products and services which are frequently linked with deceptive or misleading promotional practice.

RESTRICTED CONTENT

1. *Alcohol*

Ads which reference or promote alcohol should comply with the applicable local laws, required industry codes, licenses & approvals, guidelines, & include country and age targeting criteria that is consistent with targeting guidelines & local laws of Facebook.

2. *Dating*

Ads for online dating are allowed with written permission. Also, these should adhere to dating targeting needs and dating quality guidelines.

3. *Real Money Gambling*

Ads which facilitate or promote online money gambling, money games of skill and money lotteries that include online money casino, bingo, sports books, and poker are allowed only with written permission.

4. *State Lotteries*

Lotteries by government bodies might advertise on Facebook but provided that ads are targeted according to applicable law in which ads would be served & just target individuals in the jurisdiction.

5. *Online Pharmacies*

Ads must not encourage the sale of prescription pharmaceuticals. Also, ads for offline and online pharmacies are permitted with written permission.

6. *Supplements*

Ads which encourage acceptable herbal and dietary supplements might target those who are 18 years plus.

7. *Subscription Services*

Ads for the subscription services are subject to the requirements of subscription services.

8. *Financial Services*

Ads that promote financial services or credit card applications with the accredited institutions should clearly give sufficient disclosure about associated fees.

9. *Branded Content*

Ads that promote branded content should tag featured third-party brand, product, or business partners using a branded content tool.

10. *Student Loan*

Ads encouraging student loans should be targeted to people aged 18 years and above. Ads should not promote deceptive or misleading services.

11. *Political Advertising*

Advertisers might run political ads but the advertiser should comply with the applicable laws and authorization process.

12. *Cryptocurrency Products & Services*

   Ads might not encourage cryptocurrency and related products or services without written permission.

Video Ads

Video ads & other dynamic ad kinds should comply with the rules in the Advertising Policies such as Community Standards and the policies given below:

1. *Disruptive Content*

   Videos and similar ad forms must not use disruptive tactics including flashing screens.

2. *Entertainment-Related Restrictions*

   Ads for video game trailers, movie trailers, Television shows, and other content that's intended for mature users are only allowed with written permission for ages 18 years plus. Excessive depictions of below-mentioned contents within the ads aren't allowed:

   1. Alcohol and drugs use

   2. Adults content

   3. Violence and gore

   4. Profanity

Targeting

1. You should not use targeting options to discriminating against, disparage, harass, or provoke people or engage in some predatory advertising practice.

2. In case you're targeting your ads to the Custom Audiences then you should comply with applicable terms while creating the audience.

Positioning

. *Relevance*

Every ad component, including images, text, and other media, should be relevant to the service or product being offered and audience viewing that ad.

2. *Accuracy*

Ads should represent the service, product, company, or brand which is advertised.

3. *Landing Pages*

The services and products promoted in the ad's text should match those encouraged on a landing page. And destination sites should not link or offer any prohibited service or product.

Text in the Ad Images

Large text in the ad images might result in the ad reaching some people. Try to use less image text if possible.

Lead Ads

Advertisers should not ask questions on lead ads that request the below-mentioned kinds of information without written permission.

1. *Account Numbers*

   Ads should not request the account numbers like loyalty card numbers, flyer numbers, or telephone or cable numbers without prior written permission.

2. *Criminal History*

   Ads shouldn't request information about the arrest or criminal history without prior written permission.

3. *Financial Information*

   Ads should not ask for financial information without prior permission.

4. *Government Issued Identifiers*

   Ads should not request any government-issued identifiers such as Social Security numbers, driver's license numbers, or passport numbers without written permission.

5. *Health Information*

   Ads should not request your health information such as disabilities, physical health, medical conditions, mental health, or medical treatments without prior permission.

6. *Insurance Information*

Ads should not request the insurance information that includes recent insurance policy numbers.

7. *Political Affiliation*

Ads should not ask for information about political affiliation without written a permission.

8. *Ethnicity or Race*

Ads should not request any information about ethnicity or race without written a permission.

9. *Religion*

Ads should not ask for information about philosophical or religious beliefs without a written permission.

10. *Sexual Orientation*

Ads should not request any information about sexual orientation and information regarding the sexual life of a person without written a permission.

11. *Template Questions*

Ads should not ask for similar information which you can use as some Template Question.

12. *Membership of Trade Union*

Ads should not request information about trade Union membership without written a permission.

13. *Passwords or Usernames*

Ads should not request passwords or usernames without written permission.

Use of Brand Assets

All ads featuring Instagram or Facebook brands should be referred to Facebook Brand Resource Center and Instagram Brand Resource Center for reviewing, to ensure it adheres to brand guidelines and also downloading of approved assets.

1. *Brand Endorsement*

Ads must not imply a partnership or endorsement of any kind by Facebook, Instagram or any of its entity.

2. *Usage of Brand in Ads*

Ads should not represent Facebook in a way which makes this the most prominent or distinctive feature of a creative. The Facebook brand asset must not be edited.

3. *Copyrights and Trademarks*

All landing pages and ads must not use trademarks, copyrights, or similar marks, except permitted by Instagram Resource Center or Facebook Resource Center, or with written a permission.

4. *UI Screenshots*

Ads featuring Facebook's, Instagram's or Messenger's user interface must depict the most recent UI and how it functions in the product. If any functionality or action shown in the ad is non-functional, then it must be removed from the ad – the UI should be changed or altered in any case.

RESTRICTIONS FOR DATA USE

1. All data derived, collected or received from your Instagram or Facebook ad (i.e. "Facebook advertising data") is only shared with individuals acting on just your behalf, like a service provider.

2. Facebook ad data should only be used an aggregate and anonymous basis (as authorized by Facebook), and also to assess the effectiveness and performance of the Facebook ad campaigns.

3. Do not use Facebook ad data to edit, build, influence, append, or augment user profiles.

4. Do not transfer Facebook ad data to some ad network, data broker, ad exchange or other monetization or advertising service.

POINTS YOU MUST CONSIDER

1. Ad Policies typically apply to ads and commercial content, ads on Instagram, and ads showing within the apps on Facebook.

2. Advertisers are also responsible for complying with and understanding every applicable law and regulation.

3. We don't use personal data for the ad targeting.
4. Advertisements are actually public information. The ads might be accessed and re-shared by the users to some targeted audience, and remain accessible even after campaigns end.
5. If you're managing advertisements on behalf of some other advertisers, then every client or advertiser should be managed via individual ad accounts.
6. We can reject, remove or approve any ad for some reason, in sole discretion.
7. For the policies which require written permission, a Facebook Company or Facebook might grant such permissions.
8. The policies are subject to alter at any point in time without some notice.

CHAPTER FOUR: CREATING AND PLACING FACEBOOK ADS

Facebook ads are created in Ads Manager – Ads Manager is a helpful tool provided by Facebook to help create, edit, and view ads; you can also access the performance reports of your campaigns within ads manager.

Before creating your ads, it's important you understand or know some features Ad Manager provides. Having a good understanding of this features or structures, will help you measure your results and also carrying out test on different audiences.

Within Ads Manager, there are four tabs: Account Overview, Campaigns, Ad Sets and Ads.

Campaigns: here, you can select one objective, turn on or off ad sets, and check the performance of all your objectives.

Ad Sets: here, you can create individual ad sets for your

audience – you can also select your audience, budget, placement and schedule.

Ads: Within this ads tab, you can add copies, links and all your creatives.

Creating Ads

Within Business Manager, you can access Ads manager by clicking the drop-down menu in the upper-right corner of your Facebook page, and select "Ads Manager".

1. In ads manager, select the "Create Ad" button in the top-right corner. You'll be prompted to choose a campaign objective; the objectives are:

   - **Awareness campaign:** to generate interest in your product or service.
   - **Consideration campaigns:** let people engage in your business – you provide them with more info about your service.
   - **Conversion campaigns:** here the aim is to prompt an audience to take certain actions, like a call-to-action.

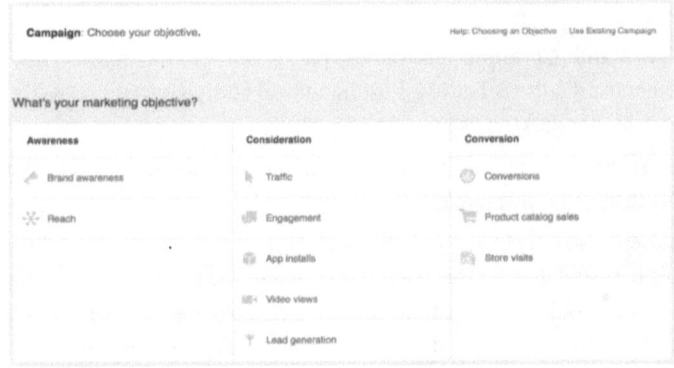

Select an objective, choose a campaign name, and create your campaign.

2. Select an audience – you can select an audience based on:

   - Location: country, state, zip, or code

- × Language
- × Age and gender
- × Interest (entertainment, fitness, food, drink etc.), and much more

3. Set a budget. Facebook allow you set how much you would like to spend on an ad. You can set or allocate media ad in 2 ways:

- × daily media spend – this is the amount of money you will spend on an ad daily
- × lifetime ad spend – the amount of money you'll spend over the duration of an ad.

4. Choose where to run your ads. You can choose to run ads on: mobile news feed, desktop news feed,
on the right side of your screen and Instagram.

- × **Desktop/Mobile News Feed:** ads will appear embedded in a user's news feed.
- × **Right-hand Column:** this option places ads on the right column of Facebook, it's the default or most traditional ad style offered. But it's only available for desktop users
- × **Instagram:** this is best suited for reaching and building brand awareness to audiences on Instagram.
- × **Audience network:** it's a partnership between Facebook and publishers. This partnership increases your reach – it lets you reach multiple people as your ads would be placed on the websites and apps of Facebook and its partners. When serving ads to audience network, you can choose the unit you would like your ad to display as; you have three options banner, native or interstitial.

5. After setting up your campaign, audience and placement, the next thing is to input your creative and copy. You first of all will have to select how your ad will display:

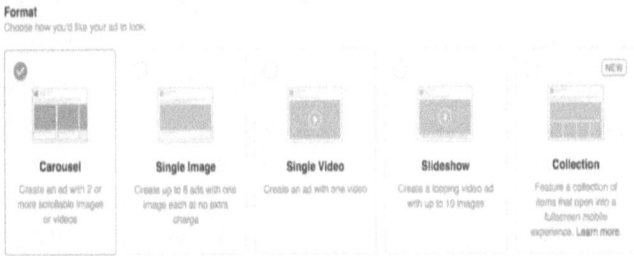

- **Carousel:** this is an ad format with 2-10 scrollable images or videos. This a format lets engages users and lets them scroll through up to ten images or videos at a time.

- **Single Image:** one of the most used and versa-

  tile ad formats, it has up to six variations of an ad displaying one image at a time.

- **Single Video:** this is an ad format with one video – using this, you can tell an engaging story to your audience.

- **Slideshow:** this is a looping video ad having up to ten images.

- **Collection:** this type of ad format combines both images and videos.

After choosing an ad format, select your image and paste/write your copy. Facebook lets you upload and test up to six different images. So, if you are not sure on what to choose, then experiment. After uploading an image, input your copy into the necessary fields (like below):

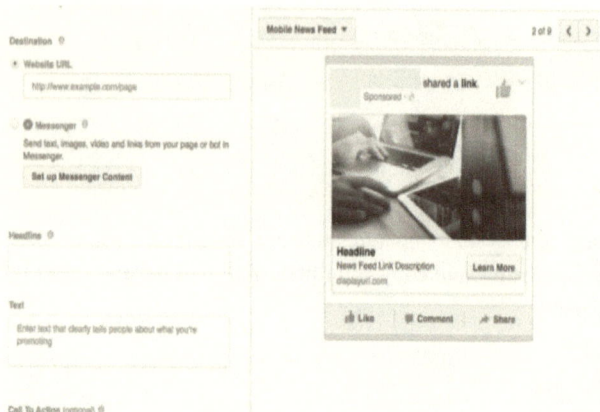

6. Once you have filled in the copy, click the "Place Order" button. Facebook will screen your ad to ensure it adheres to its advertising policies before it's approved and goes live.

Ads manager has a bunch of features that helps to manage ads, they include performance views, data exports, filters and much more.

Your Accounts

Within your account, you can view your ad account located in ads manager, and you can switch from one account to another. In ads manager, you will find your ad account number – you will need this number each time you are requesting an ad account assistance from Facebook or if you're working with a partner who wants access to your account.

Search

Below the tab in your ad account is a search tab. You will use it to search for your ads; you can search using keywords like ad name, ad set name, campaign name and campaign ID, to name a few.

Filter Options

Next to the search tab, there's a filter button. Use this to filter your ads based on what you want to view on your ads report.

Filter by Days

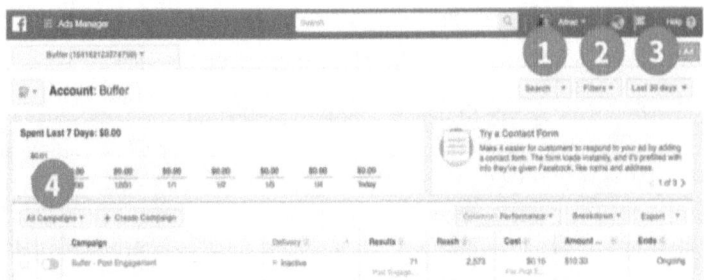

You can choose to filter which campaigns you would like to view based on days – you can view campaigns from the last 7, 14, or 30 days.

View Performance

View performance by selecting the columns tab – you can also select specific performances you would like to see, it could be based on delivery, app and video engagement.

Breakdown

This tab gives a breakdown of your campaigns. In case you need to view data for the region, gender, impression device, or country, you can find it all in the breakdown drop-down menu.

Export Data

If you need to download data for specific campaigns you've searched for, you can do so by simply exporting your files into a spreadsheet.

- × Press "Export Table Data"
- × Select file type and press "Export"
- × Download your file and your file will be saved in the selected file type.

Ads Manager Mobile Application

This app assists you in monitoring and managing you accounts when you are on the go. You can also use it to create, edit, track performance, set ad schedules and budgets, resume or pause a campaign, get push notifications and respond to alerts. The following are features which make managing accounts simpler on the go:

Home Page: It consists of quick-view summaries of your pages, accounts, and ads.
Campaigns: You could view many campaigns side by side for comparing their metrics.

Recommended Actions: This app recommends actions that helps improve ad performance.

Weekly Summary: This app gives a weekly summary of campaign performances and other information regarding ad account and creatives.

You might download this app using the following links:

App Store – *itunes.apple.com/us/app/facebook-adsmanager/id964397083*

Google Play – *play.google.com/store/apps/details?id= com.facebook.adsmanager*

If you have difficulties in creating or placing a Facebook ad, then you should practice with a boosted post. Boosted posts are the simplest ads to make – as time goes, you'll become familiar with the tools and options which you'll use when creating your ads on Ads Manager.

PLACING A BOOSTED AD

- × Create a regular page post and click Boost
- × Select an objective and CTA button
- × Select an audience and press "Run Promotion"

- Select a budget and duration – budget is a quantity that you want to spend for the duration of the campaign.
- Turn on your tracking conversions

With the myriad of targeting choices available to you on Facebook, you can target anyone and anywhere. If you need to check if an audience is big or small, use an audience size meter.

You have 2 options: you might create a new audience and/or you might upload your customer list. You've different targeting options to create a new audience: Lookalike Audience, demographics, Custom Audience, connections, behaviors, and interests. Among the numerous features offered by Facebook's Ads Manager is the ability to create lookalike audiences. A lookalike audience are Facebook users who share similar qualities to other known groups.

Demographics
When creating demographics for a target audience, you can choose from a range of options including location, language, age, and gender, to name a few.

Connections
You can target users based on connections, connections can include users who have used your app, liked your pages, and responded to your events, Also, you can exclude anyone who has some connection with your business.

Interests

There are over a hundred interest targeting options, some are: hobbies, activities, industry, entertainment, business, etc. You can target people with certain interest by inserting a keyword in the targeting search box.

Behaviors

Facebook collects data on user behaviors from their Facebook activities.

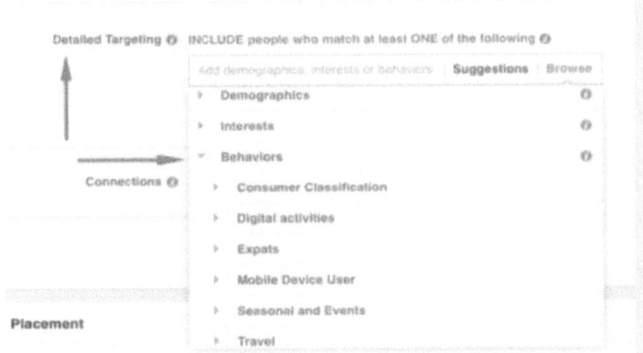

CUSTOM AUDIENCES

Custom Audience is the ad targeting tool which lets you serve ads to the current contact list, this could be a customer's list taken from sign-ups or Lead Ads. Facebook would compare your list with the data to search people on the list. There are different types of custom audience: custom audiences from your customer's list, custom audiences from your website, custom audiences from your mobile app.

To create a custom audience:

In Ads Manager, open your Facebook audiences page, and click Create a Custom Audience.

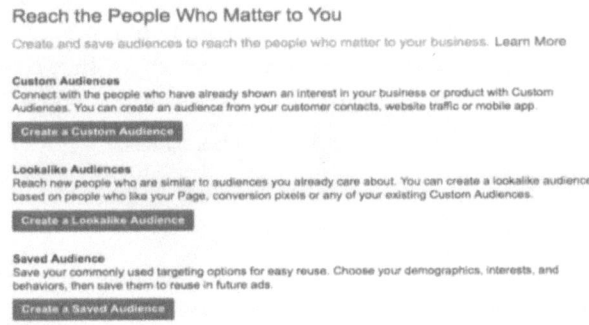

The next step depends on the type of custom audience you want to create.

CREATING A CUSTOMER LIST CUSTOM AUDIENCE

1. Click "Customer File", you'll have to choose whether to add customer information or import a list from MailChimp.

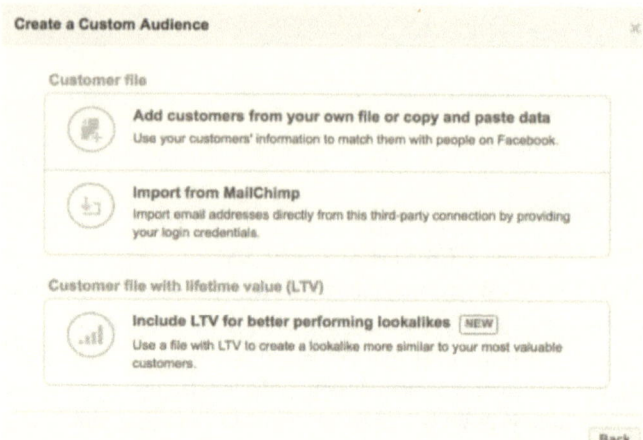

Not everyone uses MailChimp so you'll have to import some customer data, but if you do use MailChimp, you will have to enter your MailChimp login credentials and you will be prompted to take a few simple steps.

2. Accept the Custom Audience terms of service, then click "I Accept".

3. To get the most matches on your list, ensure to follow Facebook's data formatting best practices to prepare your customer list. Here are some key formatting tips:

   × Include separate columns for first and last names:

   × Ensure you include the country code on phone numbers

   × Always include a country column

4. Upload your customer data file – the file has to be in a .csv or .txt format. Next give your audience a name, and click "Next"

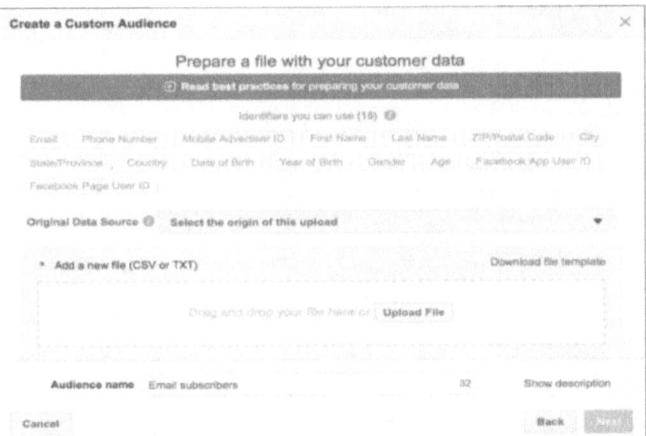

5. Facebook will prepare your newly created custom audience, it takes about half an hour.

CREATING A MOBILE APP CUSTOM AUDIENCE

1. Click "App Activity", then choose the events you want to target from the drop-down.

2. Choose a specific time frame (30 – 180 days).

3. Define your audience using details like in-app purchases or type of user's device.

4. Name your audience and click "Create Audience".

CREATING A CUSTOM AUDIENCE FROM WEBSITE VISITORS

Website visitors' custom audiences requires you install **Facebook Pixel** before it can be set up or used. Facebook Pixel is code that's placed on a website to collect data that helps in tracking conversions from Facebook ads, optimized ads, as well as building targeted audiences for future ads. I'll talk about Facebook Pixel as we proceed.

1. Select "Website Traffic", next choose the pixel you want to use to build your audience.

2. You have to choose your targets – they could be people who have visited specific pages, people who have spent a specific amount of time on your website or all website visitors. Next you'll have to set a timeframe, it can be from 30-180 days.

3. Name your audience and click "Create Audience". Wait as Facebook prepares your custom audience.

CHOOSING AD PLACEMENTS

When placing your ads on Facebook, you'll have to choose where you want the ads to be placed. Facebook gives you two options to select from: edit and automatic.

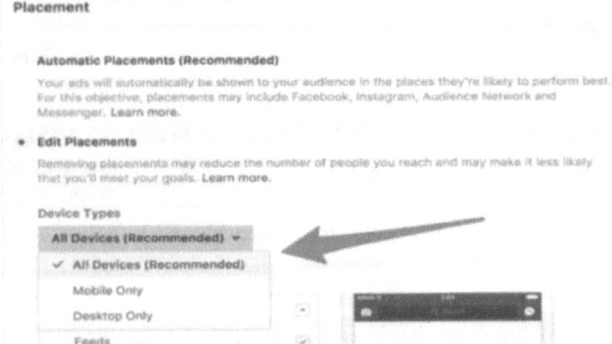

Automatic Placements: Facebook selects your recommended placements automatically so the ads are typically eligible for.

Edit Placements: Another option sees you manually select your ad placements. If you choose your selected placement, you will see a preview of how your ad will look.

AUDIENCE NETWORK

Audience network is a partnership between Facebook and various publishers. This partnership increases your reach – it lets you reach multiple people as your ads would be placed on the websites and apps of Facebook and its partners. When serving ads to audience network, you can choose the unit you would like your ad to display as; you have three options banner, native or interstitial.

Banner ads: Banner ads show like banners on the lower part of your mobile screen.

Interstitial ads: These type of ads appear during pauses in games or during the natural break in your app's flow.

Native ads: You can customize an ad's format, appearance, and size using native ad API.

You might exclude or block certain categories that you do not need appearing alongside your ad.

SETTING A BUDGET AND CREATING A SCHEDULE

When placing ads of Facebook, you will have to set a budget for your ads. A Budget is the amount of capital you are willing to pay for the period an ad runs. When selecting a budget, you have an option to select between a lifetime budget and a daily budget. A daily budget is for a 24-hour period, while a lifetime budget is for the entire duration of an ad set.

When you set a budget, it's important that you also set a schedule. There's a default option that's to run an ad set nonstop. If you choose this option, your ads run until the budget is entirely spent. There's another option that sets a start and end date. If this option is set, Facebook would run the ad for the entire period specified by the start and end date.

While selecting your optimization and bidding strategy, first think of your target. If you've the app installs ad alongside the app installs objective, selecting an app installs and ad delivery optimization would show your ad to users who installed the app. If you choose to pay for each click on your ad, the link click bidding strategy would be best. Selecting the right ad delivery optimization and bidding strategy will see you achieve your business goals.

After setting a budget and creating a schedule, you also have to choose how you will be charged (from your budget) for your ads, you have two options: you could choose to be charged for every 1,000 impressions or each time your ad is clicked.

Once payment has been made for an ad and the ad is approved, Facebook will deliver the ad to your set audience using two methods which are accelerated and standard delivery. Standard delivery will have Facebook serve the ads equally over the duration of your campaign. While accelerated delivery will see Facebook serve the ads as soon as possible.

CHAPTER FIVE: USING FACEBOOK PIXEL

Facebook Pixel is a piece of code placed on a website – it collects data that helps track conversions from Facebook ads, optimize ads and also build targeted audiences for future ads. Facebook Pixel helps provide useful information that can be used to improve ad targeting – by installing it on a website, you are able to gauge an ad's performance. Pixel tracks every user interaction with your site.

THREE BENEFITS OF USING FACEBOOK PIXEL

1. **Optimization:** Facebook Pixel collects Facebook lead and customer data, and Facebook uses these collected data to determine who to show ads to; it will show ads to those who are most likely to convert or buy something.

2. **Re-marketing:** You can use website visitor and customer data collected from Facebook Pixel to setup re-marketing campaigns to customers who have converted in the past via Facebook ads.

3. **Create a lookalike audience:** You can create a lookalike audience of your website visitors and past consumers on Facebook once your pixel tracks at least 100 conversions.

HOW TO CREATE FACEBOOK PIXEL

Step 1: Create the pixel

1. In Facebook events manager, click the hamburger icon, and select **Pixels.**

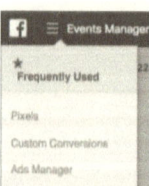

2. Click on the green "Create a Pixel" button.

Track Website Activities
Understand the actions people take after seeing your ads. Track conversions and measure your return on advertising.

Improve Your Return on Advertising
Facebook will automatically deliver ads to people more likely to take action, based on conversion data from your website.

Reach New and Existing Customers
Show ads to people based on the actions they take on your website. Create lookalike audiences to reach people similar to your best customers.

3. Name your pixel, enter the pixel URL, then click "Create"

Step 2: Add the pixel code to a site

There are various ways to set up pixel on a website depending on the platform you use:

1   Click "Manually Install the Code Yourself".

2.   Copy and paste the pixel code into the website's header code – it should be placed in <head> tag (i.e. between the<head> and </head> tag).

3. Next choose whether to use the automatic advanced matching – using this option lets you track conversions accurately and also create large custom audiences.

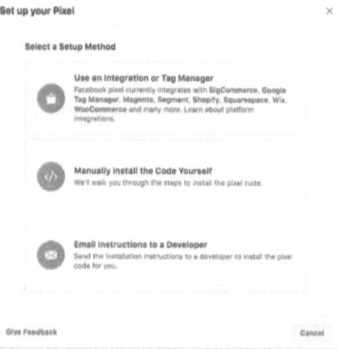

4. Now you need to ensure that pixel has been installed correctly, and you do this by entering the site's Url and clicking "Send Test Traffic". Once Facebook Pixel begins tracking an activity, click "Continue"

Name your pixel, enter the pixel URL, then click "Create"

Step 2: Add the pixel code to a site

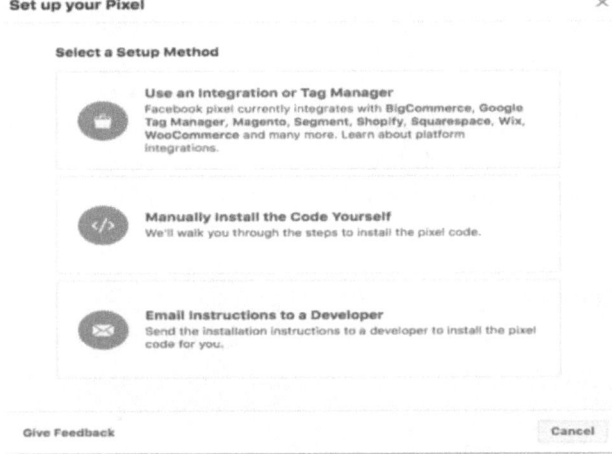

There are various ways to set up pixel on a website depending on the platform you use:

1   Click "Manually Install the Code Yourself".

2. Copy and paste the pixel code into the website's header code – it should be placed in <head> tag (i.e. between the<head> and </head> tag).

3. Next choose whether to use the automatic advanced matching – using this option lets you track conversions accurately and also create large custom audiences.

---

3 **Automatic Advanced Matching**

Use information that your customers have already provided to your business, such as their email addresses or phone numbers, to match your website's visitors to people who are on Facebook. This can help you attribute more conversions to your ads on Facebook and reach more people through remarketing campaigns. **Learn more.**

⬤ Turn on Automatic Advanced Matching

Choose the customer data you want to collect

⬤ Email

⬤ Phone Number

⬤ First and Last Name

⬤ City, State, and ZIP Code

⬤ Gender

This information will be hashed to better protect user privacy before it is sent to Facebook. Sensitive information, such as financial, health and government ID data will not be collected. **Learn more.**

---

4. Now you need to ensure that pixel has been installed correctly, and you do this by entering the site's Url and clicking "Send Test Traffic". Once Facebook Pixel begins tracking an activity, click "Continue"

---

4 **Send test traffic to your pixel**

Check the status of your pixel code by sending test traffic. If your status is shown as **Active**, your code has been installed correctly. Note that this process may take several minutes.

● No Activity Yet
  Last Received: Never

adultchildrenlivingathome.com   [Send Test Traffic]

If the status is still **No Activity Yet** after 20 minutes, your pixel code may not be installed correctly. **Get guidance** on installing your pixel. You can also visit **Test Events** in Events Manager to check your setup and troubleshoot individual pages.

Back   Give Feedback   Email Instructions   [Continue]

TROUBLESHOOTING FACEBOOK PIXEL

Facebook Pixel Helper is a must have tool – it's a Google chrome extension that

validates Facebook Pixel; it checks if pixel is correctly setup and working, as well as troubleshoot errors and boosting performance. It's free to download the Pixel Helper from Google's web store. To set up Pixel Helper:

1. Add the Facebook Pixel Helper chrome extension to your browser – to download Pixel Helper, navigate to Chrome store and search for Facebook Pixel Helper — press "Add to Chrome" — "Add extension" – once installed, the Pixel Helper icon represented by </> will appear on the upper-right corner of your Chrome browser — finally click on the Facebook helper icon in order to activate it.

2. On the page where pixel is installed, if Pixel Helper finds the pixel, the extension icon (</>) will turn blue and it will also indicate how many pixels are found on the page. If the Pixel Helper isn't working properly it will provide insightful error information that will help in correcting such errors.

CHAPTER SIX: TYPES OF ADS

There are different types of ads, some of this ads will require extra steps to set up. In this chapter, I'll guide you on creating these types of ads.

LEAD ADS

These ads are great for generating leads. A lead ad lets you gather vital information from your audience without directing them outside the Facebook platform. Lead ads helps in gathering information that you would require from potential leads, such as contact numbers, email ids etc. Lead ads are super-efficient and superior to normal site forms for these reasons:

1. Lead ads are built with the mobile user in mind.
2. Lead ads pre-fill forms with the users' information.
3. Lead ads have a conversion ratio of 50%, which is better than site forms.

Lead ads are eligible for Instagram feeds, Facebook desktop and mobile news feed. To set up lead ads:

1. Press lead generation — continue

Facebook Tests Ads Containing Multiple Products | AdvertiseMint

Facebook is currently testing ads that contain multiple products within the news feed.

1. Select a Facebook page
2. Create your target audience

3. Select placements
4. Set your budget and schedule
5. Select your format
6. Input your copy or text – it should give your audience a clear understanding regarding your business and offer.
7. Create your form
8. Press "New Form" from ad level
9. Press Questions - Custom Questions - Add Custom Question – Conditional.
10. Upload the spreadsheet and write your questions – while writing the questions, ensure all questions are worded in a way that's applicable to every possible answer. After you have created the form, you submit your Lead Ad for approval by Facebook

Personalizing Advertising & Marketing with the Messenger Ads

The Messenger Ads can directly send customers to the conversation window as they click your ad. Here is how to make your Messenger Ads.

1. Select the objective – some objectives include: catalog sales, traffic, brand awareness, conversions, Messages, app installs, and reach are eligible for such kind of ad.
2. Select Messenger for the traffic
3. Select your target audience
4. Select the placements
5. Select your budget and Select your Facebook & Instagram page
6. Select the format
7. Upload images
8. Add pixel, text, and CTA button
9. Set up your Messenger
10. Create your welcome experience: the standard template
11. Next create your welcome experience, the custom template — type the text greeting and personalize your message. You can choose to personalize

messages using the first name, last name or full name. After that, choose your responses list – they should be relevant to your business goals. You can select a response which would answer general questions.

Note that using the custom template lets you customize greeting with videos and photos, to include buttons which send users to your site, and to create automatic replies hence you may respond to your customers even if you're far from your phone or computer.

While creating buttons, you've to give action, label, and site URL. A label is the CTA button which encourages your customers to take the action. Action options include "Send a postback" and "Open a website." Unless you've a Chabot, choose the 1st option that's "Open a website" and add your site URL where you want customers to go when they click your label. After setting up messages, submit your ad for review.

This lets you use videos and photos to customize greetings, also include buttons which would send users to your site and also create automatic replies; automatic replies would assist in responding to your customers when you are away from your phone or computer.

Ensure you add action, label and site URL to the buttons. A label is a call-to-action (CTA) button that encourages potential customers to take a certain action. Some action options include: "Send a postback" and "Open a website". If you don't have a Chabot, use the option "Open a website".

Sell Your Products: Broad Dynamic Product Ads, Dynamic Product Ads, and Collection Ads

Certain formats work with certain targets. When selling a product, several formats are known to work well, these formats advertise your products and target audience in an efficient way.

Dynamic Product Ads

Dynamic Product ads advertise products from a product catalog by making alterations according to a customer's recent sales-funnel stage. These ads usually contain up to ten images and videos which customers can scroll through. It features relevant products to customers in certain stages of the sales funnel via a single image ad format. You can promote your products in just one ad, reach your audience on devices they use, set up the campaigns once, and show your ads with products that customers are more likely to purchase. For creating Dynamic Product Ad, you should have the following items.

Online Product Catalog: You'll use existing catalog from some online shopping portals. Product catalog made on Facebook should have a name, product ID, description, availability, landing page URL, and image URL.

Facebook Pixel: Pixel is an important element as it tracks the web activity and displays the relevant products.

To create the dynamic product ad:

1. Select product catalog sales objective.
2. Select product set and audience
3. Select placement
4. Set budget & schedule
5. Choose your optimization

To optimize an ad for a good delivery, you have three options:

Link clicks: Facebook will show your ad to people who will click on them.

Impressions: Facebook will show your ad to as many people as possible.

Conversion events: Facebook will deliver your ad to people who take action as they view some product from the catalog.

BROAD DYNAMIC PRODUCT ADS

Dynamic Product Ad works by re-targeting customers who interact with a business. It prevents advertisers from getting new customers. When you need to re-target and get new customers you can use Broad Dynamic Product Ad which targets a large audience.

1. Create a Dynamic Product Ad.

2. At ad set level, under the Create New in Audience section, press

3. Select target gender, location, and age.

4. Press Show Advanced Options. Now, refine the audience and exclude users who take less action on the ads.

Exclude people who bought: The ad will not be shown to those who already bought your products.

No exclusions: You do not exclude anyone from viewing your ads.

Create the custom exclusion: The ad will not appear to those depending on the rules that you specify.

Collection Ads

Collection Ads lets you attach several product photos to the image ad or video in the News Feed. If you create a Collection Ad, you are combining both the Single Video Ad and Dynamic Product Ad. To create a collection ad:

1. Select traffic or conversions as an objective

2. Select where you have to direct the traffic

3. Select your audience

4. Select the placements

5. Set the budget and schedule

6. Connect pages

7. Select collection format and template – you can choose from three templates: showcase your business, sell products or get new customers

8. Upload media and destination URL

9. Here, you'll choose a cover video or photo. Next, give the destination URL. The URL would bring customers to the landing page just after clicking your ad

10. Add your product catalog – select a particular order, products from the catalog or products that you enter manually would appear in the ad

11 Create CTA Button and include a CTA URL

12. Submit your ad for review by Facebook.

Dynamic Creative Ads

Dynamic Creative Ads can appear as image or video, and they automatically change appearance. Here's how they work: you insert creatives; the ad then combines these creatives automatically to create different ads. The ads deliver variations, look for the perfect performing version, and continue delivering these best-performing ads.

For creating a Dynamic Creative Ad, select any of these objectives: conversion, brand awareness, lead generation, reach, video views, traffic, and app installs. Next, select quick creation workflow.

1. Click the create button
2. Create a campaign. Press Save to Draft.
3. Turn on Dynamic Creative at your ad set level
4. At your ad set level, select one option from the following: Ad with a Video or Image or Ad with Multiple Image in the Carousel
5. Upload texts, descriptions, and headlines
6. Preview the ad variations
7. Save or publish ads

Slideshow Ads

Slideshow Ads provide two key benefits: First, it works great in countries which have slow net connections. Slideshow ad loads easily and quickly as it's lightweight. Second, Slideshow ad is a perfect alternative to the video ads. The ad format has an illusion of a video.

1. Select your objective
2. Select your audience
3. Select your placement
4. Select your budget & schedule
5. Connect the pages
6. Select Slideshow as the format

7. Select your media – if you upload music to the slideshow, you should use any one of these formats: OGG, WAV, FLAC, MP3, and M4A.

8. Add your pixel tracking, text, and URL

360 Video Ads

360 video ads are rarely used because they are expensive, cost time and technical skills to set up. 360 video ads require special cameras such as Allie camera, Samsung Gear 360, Giroptic 360 cam, RICOH THETA S and 360Fly.

Currently, one cannot upload a 360 video to ads manager to create a 360 video ad, but it can be uploaded to a page's timeline and the post can be boosted until. In order to use a 360 video, the video will have to be recorded using a spherical or 360 camera system that adds 360 metadata. You can add 360 metadata before uploading the video.

When uploading a video without metadata, follow the below steps:

1. Click camera icon under text box of the status update and choose a video to upload
2. Click Advanced tab
3. Click "This Video Was Recorded in 360 Format"

4. Press 360 Controls tab

5. Now publish – you'll will get a notification which states that your video could display in 360. Continue with the below steps to finalize your 360 video.

6. Click notification - Edit Video Page

7. Press Enable 360 encoding

8. Click Save

When the video is on page's timeline, click "Boost Post" on the post's bottom-right side. 360 video would have a 360 icon for distinguishing itself from the regular video. Device requirements for a 360 video ad:

iPhone

- × Hardware must be iPad 2 or newer or 4S or newer

- × OS must be iOS7 or new

- × An App must be Facebook iOS app

Android

- × Hardware must be of 2012 or newer

- × Os must be Android version 4.3 or newer

- × And you must use the Facebook app for android

On web

Browsers must be Google Chrome or Firefox.

CHAPTER SEVEN: BUSINESS MANAGER

In the preceding chapters, I have talked about business manager, in this chapter, I'll give an in-depth view of Facebook's Business Manager.

Business Manager is a great tool used for analyzing and re-targeting – it's used to manage ad assets, such as pages, mobile apps, ad accounts, product catalogs and Instagram accounts. Business Manager simplifies handling of assets – all assets are easily accessible in a single place and you can grant access to people working with you. There are plenty features which are vital in Business Manager; these features will be discussed in this section.

CAMPAIGN PLANNER

Campaign Planner is a toll offered by Business Manager used to estimate the frequency and reach of a campaign, this depends on ad placements, budget and the target audience you select. After plans for the campaigns have been created, you can then compare the campaigns with one another, as well as share the campaign predictions with colleagues. To share results, click on the share button on the upper-right side of your screen. You can also share important data via email or shareable link; it can also be downloaded in a .csv file.

If you like the result, you can purchase the plan by pressing "Reserve for Purchase", all plans you create will be shared automatically. You can check if a plan is up to date by viewing the status represented in three indicators or symbols: red triangle, green circle and gray circle. A green circle means it's updated, gray circle shows it's not updated and a red triangle means there's an error.

AUTOMATED RULES

These are rules created by Facebook to automate the most common tasks – these rules are based on the data from campaigns, and are automatically applied to ad campaigns.

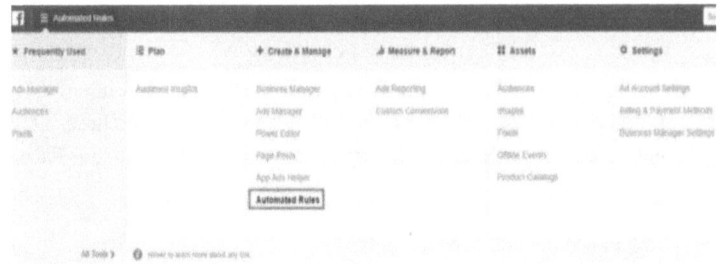

Apply Rule: You can might apply a rule to active campaigns, ads, or ad sets.

Action: What would happen if a condition is met? The options are turned off, adjust manual bid, adjust budget, or send notification.

Condition: It triggers an automated rule. You'll choose from the list of items including daily spend, cost per result, lifetime spends, results, and frequency, among many others. You can then set thresholds to something equal, greater than, or lesser than the number you want. If a campaign, ad, or ad set reaches the threshold in the chosen time range, then the automated rule would complete an action that you have selected.

AUDIENCE INSIGHTS

It's a tool that helps one understand their audience's behaviors and interest. It aids in targeting ads and also provides exclusive reports on purchase activity, demographics, location, behaviors, lifestyle, language, interests and Facebook activities.

Here is how to use the audience insights:

1. First, Open Audience insights
2. Select an audience – when selecting an audience, you'll be given 3 options: Custom Audience, everyone on Facebook, and people connected to your page.

3. Set the parameters – ensure you only define users whose insights you see. You can select an audience based on interests, country, gender, and age.
4. Explore the data – you may look at multiple parts of the demographics such as age, lifestyle, gender, household information, relationship status, and job title.

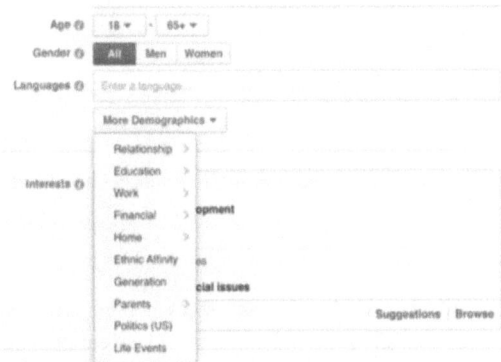

Audience insights helps in knowing one's target audience. Filtering and selecting a target audience takes some strategy – it's recommended to target users who have shown interests in your business.

DELIVERY INSIGHTS

These are insights that can be accessed when viewing ads sets in Ads Manager, it shows also displays issues with ad's delivery – this piece of information will aid in diagnosing delivery problems and help improve results. Delivery insights includes information like analysis describing reasons for delivery volatility in ways which the issues can be solved or addressed. While accessing the delivery insights, you'll see 3 tabs which contain information regarding the performance of the ad set.

Activity History	Auction Overlap	Audience Saturation
Date		Impressions
04/26/2017		
	Impressions	
04/25/2017	The number of times your ads were viewed.	
04/24/2017		20,386
04/23/2017		17,718
04/22/2017		19,319
04/21/2017		18,646

Activity: It shows you actions that are taken on the particular ad set just like deliveries and updates.

Audience saturation: It occurs if an audience views your ads several times & refuses to give a response to them.

Auction overlap: The auction overlap occurs if you target an overlapping audience that makes you bid against yourself.

Delivery insights can be accessed in two ways:

- **A business notification:** If an ad set faces some performance shift then Facebook will notify you. This notification would appear on the Ads Manager's top-right corner.
- **Ads Manager:** All ad sets with the performance shift have "See Delivery Insights" link.

CREATIVE HUB

It's a platform where the advertisers can test create, share, review and test ad mockups. It's mainly focuses on mobile ads and explores new ways that advertisers can create attractive and compelling ads that are compressed within the mobile screen.

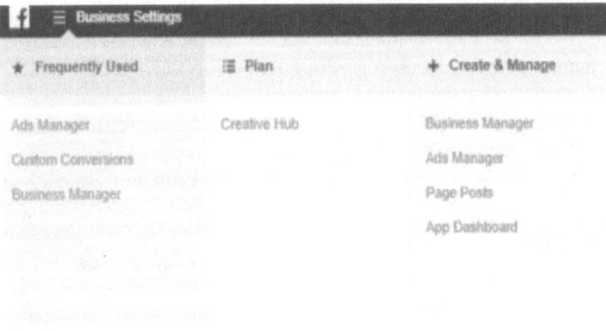

Using creative hub:

- You can browse through the ad creatives that are designed by the agencies and brands at the Hub's gallery which is located under "Get Inspired Tab."
- You can preview mockups in each available ad format on Instagram and Facebook.
- You can save mockups.
- You can collaborate and exchange ideas with teams.
- You can generate a URL of the mockup for sending to clients and colleagues.
- You can check whether the image is according to Facebook's 20% text rule.

ADS REPORTING

Ads reporting is a tool that can help store all saved reports. To navigate through the ads reporting page:

- Press the ad, campaigns, or ad sets to run your report. Click a category that you need to get your report on
- Next, press "Export" — "Create Custom Report"

CUSTOM CONVERSIONS

Create a Custom Conversion

Pixel   Charlie Lawrance All Sites Pixel
     Pixel ID ▄▄▄▄▄▄▄▄▄▄

Rule   Include traffic that meets the following conditions:

URL contains ▾

✓ URL contains   and
URL equals

Category   Event ▾

Choose the category that best describes the rule that you're defining. Selecting a category helps Facebook learn how to optimise advert delivery for the custom conversion that you're creating

Custom conversions lets you optimize and track user specific actions even without adjusting the existing pixel code, they also let you track a conversion event based on the URL string. It is a process which needs replacing pixels placed on your final page after required action is finished. With custom conversions, you could enter the URL of your page that you will mark as the conversion, and Facebook would track every user who visits that page.

IMAGES AND PIXELS

In the drop-down menu in Business Manager, under the assets section, there's an option labeled "mages" – it contains an image page that has all the images that have been uploaded for different ads. Below the assets tab, there's an option labeled "Pixels" – clicking it directs to a page which holds information regarding all pixels. Here, you can view a graph that notifies if a pixel is set and also a list which consists of the domains, URLs and devices that a pixel was fired from.

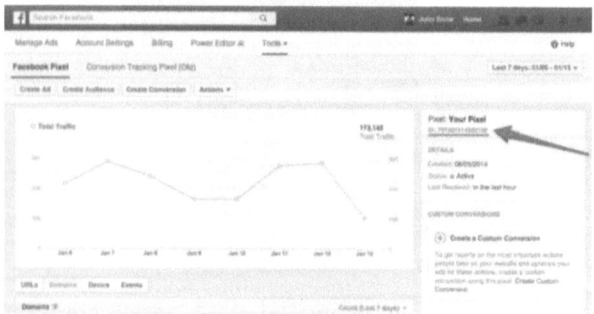

Page Post

This section has all published page posts. You can create and delete you posts from here.

App Dashboard

It consists of all advertised apps – within this dashboard, you can view the app ID and status.

Monetization Manager

It's a tool that helps in tracking an audience network and also managing its monetization. Within monetization manager, you can manage ads and ads placement, analyze ad performance and optimize revenue.

Analytics

It contains all analytics for pixels, groups, pages, and apps. Analytics information contains monthly new users, monthly active users, & monthly revenue. You can visit this page for monitoring the performance of assets.

Events Manager

It contains your assets that are related to the event tracking. You can also access your partner integrations, pixels, custom conversions, offline events, and app events.

CTR

CTR or click through rate is the rate at which an ad is clicked. It's represented as a percentage, and you'll use this percentage to figure out whether your ad is relevant to your audience. A low CTR indicates that an ad isn't attracting users, and a high CTR indicates the opposite.

Cost per Link Click (CPC)

This is the average cost for every click on a link. It can be calculated by dividing the total amount spent on the ad by the link clicks.

Impressions

Impressions indicates the number of times an ad appears on user's screen – if a user, scrolls down the News Feed, come upon the ad, Facebook will count this instance as 1 impression. If that user scrolls back up to view your ad, that also counts as 1 impression.

Cost per 1,000 Impressions (CPM)

It's the average cost for every thousand impressions. It can be calculated by dividing the total amount spent by the impressions, and multiplied by one thousand, i.e.: total amount spent / impressions x 1,000

Cost per Result

This simply shows the cost per result. This result is an outcome relying on the objectives that you elected for the ad. It's calculated by dividing the amount that you spent by your results.

Website Purchase Return on Ad Spend

This tells you how much capital you make on every dollar spent – it also tells you whether an ad is generating revenue or not.

CHAPTER EIGHT: SPLIT TESTING AND SCALING

Split testing or A/B testing is a process that involves testing more than one at a time using different ad elements on each of the ads – in split testing, one tests each ad for performance, and compares the performance results of all ads. The purpose of testing is to determine which ad type works best.

When testing ad elements, avoid testing too many variables, as doing this will make it hard to determine which or what variable causes an ad to do well. A better way to test an ad will be to create one ad for each variable you would like to test. A valid split testing result should have at least 100 conversions for each ad variation.

You should leverage Facebook Analytics in your test – Facebook Analytics is a tool provided by Facebook within Business Manager. It contains information about a customer's interaction with the business across an app, website, Messenger and Facebook page. Facebook Analytics needs customers' information from any of these four channels: website, app, Facebook page and Messenger.

OVERVIEW OF FACEBOOK ANALYTICS

Facebook Analytics provides metrics and tools which help in measuring ad performance as well as optimizing ads. Metrics provided by Facebook Analytics are:

Key Metrics: contains vital metrics such as numbers for new conversations, unique users, active conversations, and new users. These metrics indicates your ad performance.

Active Users for Last 1 Day: It contains all unique users who have been active on the site within the last 24 hours.

Active Users, By Hour: shows the time and day when the visitors are active on the website.

Active Users: It shows your active daily, monthly, and weekly users. This is important information in keeping the track of your site traffic.

People: Demographics of the most active people, this metric consists of the age, country, and gender of the visitors.

Top Reacted Posts: These contain page posts which have most reactions. The information helps in determining which posts actually resonate with the target audience.

Top Shared Posts: This is a metric for your Facebook pages, it shows which posts users have shared the most. Such information can be used to determine which kind of posts is popular among the page followers.

Top Commented Posts: It shows posts with the most comments. This information helps in identifying posts which resonate the most with followers.

Age & Gender: It highlights the demographics of a page's followers or web visitors. This information can be used to know one's target audience.

Country: It shows countries where a page followers or web visitors reside. You'll use this information in order to improve the ad targeting.

Post Reactions: It shows the number of times your audience reacted to the Facebook posts.

Post Shares: It shows the number of times your audience shared a posts.

Post Comments: It shows the number of times your audience commented on a posts.

Messages Sent: It shows the number of times you've messaged users on Messenger

Messages Received: It shows the number of times your audience messaged you on Messenger. It helps determine if one should pursue a Messenger campaign.

Some tools provided by Facebook Analytics are:

User Retention: This tool is used to determine how users are retaining information about a brand or product.

Breakdowns: This breaks down groups & organizes your data in accordance with the parameters that you select.

Events: it consists of your custom and pre-defined events. These are actions which users take in the channels. This tool consists of event metrics including count, description, unique users, and value.

Event Debugging: You can use this tool for checking whether the events are correctly logging or not.

Lifetime Value: This tool consists of important data of the lifetime value chart.

SCALING FACEBOOK ADS

The difference between small time marketers or advertisers and the big shots is SCALE. Scaling an ad simply means increasing your budget – if you need your ads to bring in bigger results, then you have to scale. Scaling is a very powerful, at the same time it can be disastrous, so before you scale ensure your ads is at least 25-30% profitable. Here's how to scale (it's pretty simple): launch your ad optimize your campaign to at least a 25% profit rate or margin — scale.

Four tips to help in scaling an ad:

1. Adjust your budget
2. Expand your target audience and increase the size of your lookalike audience
3. Be creative with your ads
4. A/B test your ads

CHAPTER NINE: THE PSYCHOLOGY OF ADS

As you advertise your products or services, people will buy.

The reason they buy whatever it is you sell can be attributed to what is referred to as *"The Five Ps of Marketing"* - these 5 Ps are: people, product, promotion, price and placement. The 5 Ps of marketing are further explained below:

People

People are influenced to make purchases by people, these influencers can be public figures or celebrities, and friends. People are more likely to buy a product if it has been recommended by a friend, family or celebrity.

Product

People are more likely to buy from you if you have a quality product that meets their requirements, and also if

your product is better than the competition. When placing Facebook ads, you have to show customers that your product is better than your competitors.

Promotion

Promotion entices people to buy a product – it brings your product to the attention of potential buyers and it also urges them to take an action (and this action is to buy what you offer).

Price

Price can make or break a deal. Customers are more likely to buy from you if the price is fair.

Placement

Strategic placement of an ad or store location is one more element that makes a customer purchase a product. You can create a store location ad to target audience within the store location.

Beyond the 5 Ps, there are also some elements that push a customer to purchase a product or offer, or better still take a specific action. Some of them are:

Evoking Emotions

Emotions influence lots of human decisions. An emotion evoking ad (that's of high quality, eye catching and telling a compelling story) can stop a user mid-scroll – this also seals their attention and makes them buy.

Scarcity

Scarcity is known to work well alongside sale discounts – if people think that a product is limited in stock or low in supply, they are spurred to make a purchase quickly before it runs out of stock.

Kinship

People are more likely to respond to an ad if they think or feel it relates to them. So, when placing ads, ensure you relate to your target audience and try and speak their language.

Urgency

Creating urgency is a way to make users complete certain actions. An example of urgency is an ad campaign that announces a "24 hr sale" or a limited stock available.

An average Facebook users' purchase intent is influenced by a host of factors. We have looked at the 5 Ps of marketing and other elements that influence user purchase decisions, some of these other factors are ad copy, image and video.

Copy

This is the core of your ad, it tells users what your ad is all about and what you want them to do. A copy can break or make an ad. An ad copy appears in 3 areas: a description under its headline, a text above its image, and a headline under its image.

An effective copy is one that is compelling, relevant to the product or service and provides a solution to the issue it highlights. A good tip when creating ad copy is to know your target audience. Two tips to help you create a good and effective copy:

- Know your target audience – without a clear idea of who your audience is, you won't be able to create a copy that's specific to such audience.
- Your copy shouldn't be too *salesy*. What this means is that the primary reason a user is online or logged on Facebook is to connect and socialize, and not to buy. So ads that are screaming *buy buy buy* will annoy them. So, your ads should take a mild selling approach – instead of selling or look like you are selling, bring up a problem and also provide a solution to the problem.

Images

Images are the most prominent and visible element of any ad. Your images should catch a user's attention and also be able to stop a user mid-scroll.

You can test different images that features objects and people. When you select feature objects instead of people in an, don't forget to add or feature your product or service.

Video

Videos are good for storytelling – this form of moving creative lets an audience watch your story whether the story is regarding your product, service, or brand. Whether on Facebook or Instagram stories, keep the following points in mind to ensure the video is effective:

- Try and keep it short, at least a minute
- Go straight to the point

- Ensure to make the sound off video as most people watch videos without sound
- Remove unnecessary sounds or captions to make it comprehensible

CHAPTER TEN; CONCLUSION

When placing Facebook ads, the results sometimes may not be what you expected, but being consistent and trying new strategies will make the difference. Once you begin getting positive results, rinse and repeat the process over again. Also, you would want to increase your budget to increase your reach and results. For any objective you choose, Facebook will optimize the ad for that objective. Also, there's something known as the learning phase – the learning phase is Facebook's way of trying to determine how to generate the best results from your ad campaigns. In this learning phase, your ad is showed or served to different people within your target audience so as to determine who is most likely to take your specific or desired actions.

The learning phase is more of an experimental process,

so it's accurate to say that the results one gets during this period is likely to be worse than the results you will get once Facebook has finally optimized your ad or campaign. Also, this phase usually lasts for 50 optimization events, and this is determined by Facebook and your selected objective.

Facebook Advertising is a sure-fire way to promote and sell products and services to a global audience.

www.ingramcontent.com/pod-product-compliance
Lightning Source LLC
Chambersburg PA
CBHW030952240526
45463CB00016B/2519